Blastoff! Beginners are developed by literacy experts and educators to meet the needs of early readers. These engaging informational texts support young children as they begin reading about their world. Through simple language and high frequency words paired with crisp, colorful photos, Blastoff! Beginners launch young readers into the universe of independent reading.

Sight Words in This Book

a	from	look	she	two
and	get	new	sit	
at	good	on	the	
big	in	one	they	
eat	is	out	this	
find	jump	play	too	

This edition first published in 2022 by Bellwether Media, Inc.

No part of this publication may be reproduced in whole or in part without written permission of the publisher. For information regarding permission, write to Bellwether Media, Inc., Attention: Permissions Department, 6012 Blue Circle Drive, Minnetonka, MN 55343.

Library of Congress Cataloging-in-Publication Data

Names: Rathburn, Betsy, author.
Title: Baby pandas / Betsy Rathburn.
Description: Minneapolis, MN : Bellwether Media, 2022. | Series: Too cute! | Includes bibliographical references and index. | Audience: Ages 4-7 | Audience: Grades K-1
Identifiers: LCCN 2021040729 (print) | LCCN 2021040730 (ebook) | ISBN 9781644875766 (library binding) | ISBN 9781648345876 (ebook)
Subjects: LCSH: Pandas--Infancy--Juvenile literature.
Classification: LCC QL737.C27 R375 2022 (print) | LCC QL737.C27 (ebook) | DDC 599.78913/92--dc23
LC record available at https://lccn.loc.gov/2021040729
LC ebook record available at https://lccn.loc.gov/2021040730

Text copyright © 2022 by Bellwether Media, Inc. BLASTOFF! BEGINNERS and associated logos are trademarks and/or registered trademarks of Bellwether Media, Inc.

Editor: Amy McDonald   Designer: Jeffrey Kollock

Printed in the United States of America, North Mankato, MN.

Table of Contents

A Baby Panda!	4
Cute Climbers	6
All Grown Up!	20
Baby Panda Facts	22
Glossary	23
To Learn More	24
Index	24

A Baby Panda!

Look at the baby panda. Hello, cub!

Cute Climbers

Newborn cubs start out tiny and pink.
They grow quickly.

newborn

Cubs **nurse**.
They drink milk from mom.

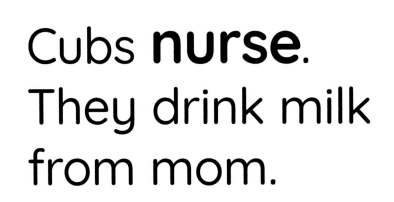

nursing

Cubs get bigger. They leave the **den**.

den

Cubs play.
This one jumps on mom!

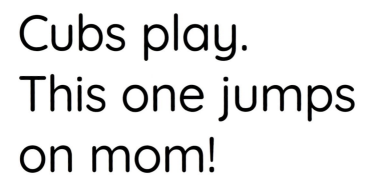

Cubs climb.
This one sits
in a tree.

Cubs eat a lot. **Bamboo** tastes good.

Cubs sleep a lot, too. They nap in trees!

All Grown Up!

This cub is two.
She finds
a new home.
Goodbye, mom!

Baby Panda Facts

Panda Life Stages

newborn   cub   adult

A Day in the Life

play   climb   eat

Glossary

bamboo

a plant that pandas eat

den

a home for some animals

newborn

just born

nurse

to drink mom's milk

To Learn More

ON THE WEB

FACTSURFER

Factsurfer.com gives you a safe, fun way to find more information.

1. Go to www.factsurfer.com.

2. Enter "baby pandas" into the search box and click 🔍.

3. Select your book cover to see a list of related content.

Index

bamboo, 16, 17
climb, 14
den, 10
drink, 8
eat, 16
grow, 6
home, 20
jumps, 12
milk, 8

mom, 8, 12, 20
nap, 18
newborn, 6
nurse, 8, 9
panda, 4
play, 12
sits, 14
sleep, 18
tree, 14, 18

The images in this book are reproduced through the courtesy of: Eric Isselee, front cover, pp. 3, 4, 5, 18, 22 (cub, adult); Xinhua/ Alamy, pp. 6, 22 (newborn); Eric Baccega/ SuperStock, pp. 6-7; Mitsuaki Iwago/ SuperStock, pp. 8-9; Adrian Warren/ SuperStock, p. 10; Keren Su/ China Span/ Alamy, pp. 10-11; ZSSD/ SuperStock, pp. 12-13; Dmitry Rukhlenko, pp. 14-15; dibrova, p. 16; Pascale Gueret, pp. 16-17, 20-21, 22 (eat); Lejanvre Philippe/ Alamy, pp. 18-19; Wonderly Imaging, p. 22 (play); Hung Chung Chih, p. 22 (climb); Iakiv Pekarskyi, p. 23 (bamboo); Piotr Krzeslak, p. 23 (den); agefotostock/ Alamy, p. 23 (newborn); dandumrong, p. 23 (nurse).